Char.

Change Room

Mark Cochrane

For Ryan —
With thanks for "Dumbhead"
& for moving this book
forward — I'm grateful
that we've met.
Best, [signature]
May 18/2000

Talonbooks

2000

Talonbooks
#104—3100 Production Way
Burnaby, British Columbia, Canada V5A 4R4

Typeset in Adobe Garamond Condensed and printed and bound in Canada by Hignell Printing Ltd.

First Printing: April, 2000

Talonbooks are distributed in Canada by General Distribution Services, 325 Humber College Blvd., Toronto, Ontario, Canada M9W 7C3; Tel.:(416) 213-1919; Fax:(416) 213-1917.

Talonbooks are distributed in the U.S.A. by General Distribution Services Inc., 4500 Witmer Industrial Estates, Niagara Falls, New York, U.S.A. 14305-1386; Tel.:1-800-805-1083; Fax:1-800-481-6207.

Canadä

The publisher gratefully acknowledges the financial support of the Canada Council for the Arts; the Government of Canada through the Book Publishing Industry Development Program; and the Province of British Columbia through the British Columbia Arts Council for our publishing activities.

Canadian Cataloguing in Publication Data

Cochrane, Mark, 1965-
  Change room

  Poems.
  ISBN 0-88922-432-3

  I. Title.
PS8555.O267C52 2000   C811'.54   C00-910363-5
PR9199.3.C548C52 2000

to tell of bodies
transformed
into new shapes
you gods, whose power
worked all transformations,
help the poet's breathing ...

Contents

III.   Locker Room

IV.   Line Jumpers

Book of Hours

Whitman would have wept
to witness these men: arms like great
challah loaves, cumulous
triceps & delts, & each
with his notebook, his diary
spiral-bound or clothed in paisley, each
taking the daily ledger
of his flesh, sets & reps, spreadsheets
of accomplishment & the dull
disciplines of the wide back—

To pass
among them, I train on the weights
with passable diligence
while in the close-ruled pages of my book
the lines bulge with body notes, the measure
of other men's muscle, I loafe
& observe their jerking, straining, their
bursts of breath, I take in
the smell of them, & the smithy music
the cast plates make—

I am a spy
in this chamber of iron, dance-thump & chains
& in my book, you boys, I am kneading
oil into your depilated
pecs, in my book
I am wrapping your fingers, callused & chalky,
lewd & protuberant from their palm-gloves,
around the flush diameter of myself
to squeeze—

Clustered & bent at the water fountain
you cannot guess at this

but in my book, Titans, I will stitch nine signatures
down your knotted spines
to collate
musky secrets—yours
with mine

(in the showers with me
you shall not guess at this

& there,
on that grid of wet tile
I will lay down my treasons
as devotions, I will betray men
the way mosaic text
betrays god

      —in my book, its cover stained
      with back-sweat from the abs mat,
      the benches, with ass-sweat
      from the leg press,
      I will kneel
      before manhood
      like a man, & pronounce your glories
      as one who renounces, & wholly believes.

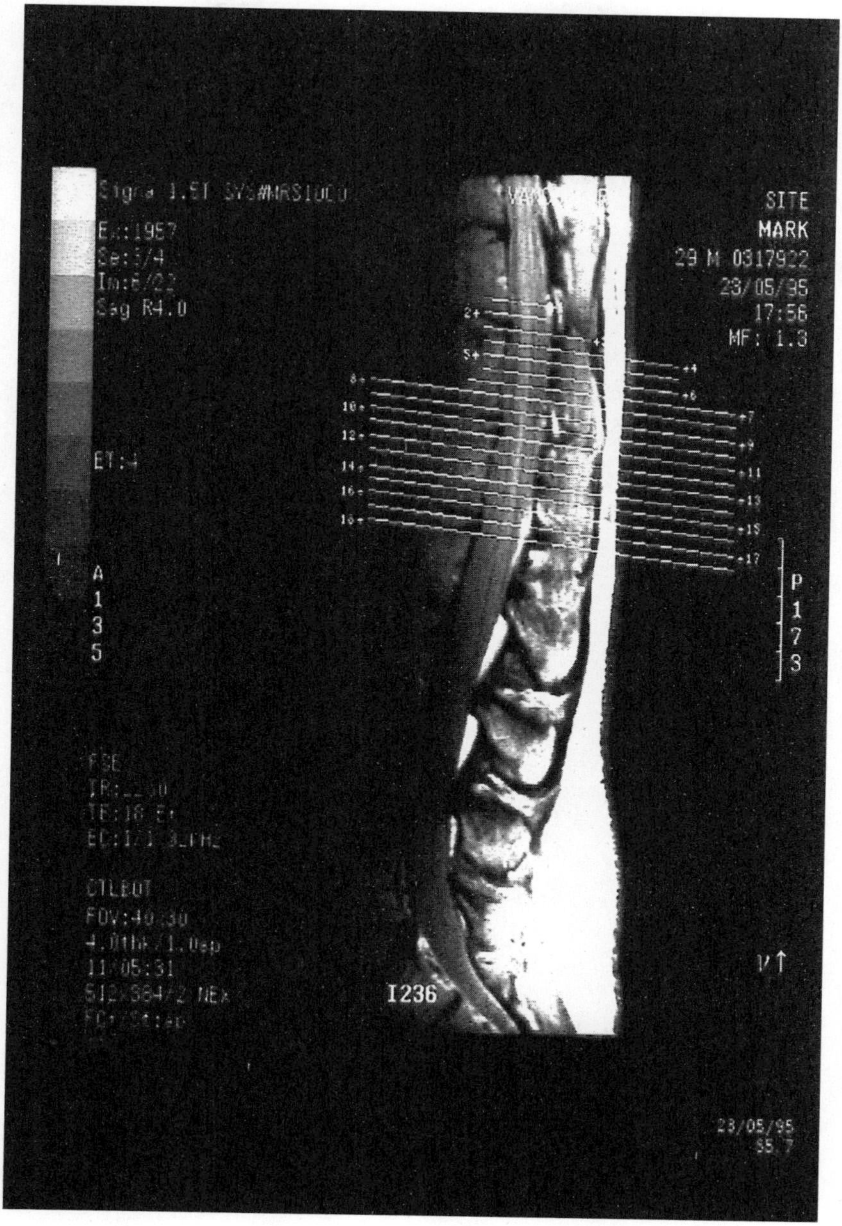
SITE
MARK
29 M 0317922
23/05/95
17:56
MF: 1.3
Se:3/4
Im:6/22
Sag R4.0
ET:4
I236
23/05/95

[*sic*]

*Health in literature, no less than in
life, is very boring …*

— John Bentley Mays

Gulf Island Panic

I wake, verb to *funeral*, with tourniquet
gut, anaconda that wrings
rabbit, gluts on dishcloth—

froth: as if. Writhe, rise
harrowed by life, knot life, low flesh
clenched to the pubis

in leather nubs, wizened gargoyle
with a slit nose, recoiling—
actually gag just arching

lips to breathe. Good morning,
shoulder buzz, fish gasp—
coccyx, cardiac, wherefore art

/ but sternum winch, rib-spread
& sigh again: two breaths
time for a drink. But wait—

I love the lover I live with.
I have everything I thought I wanted
& all of this has happened before.

I am spoiled, anxiety
my *decadent affliction*
I whine in these black jeans: *Die*

the piglet body squeals or
I will it, no difference
now the evil dribbles in the ear

like a bad brother, sparks
when I pee, Or: *surge*, spine tor-
qued of klutz rutting but

the wires are clean, not a herniated
disc on the screen: the "body" declines
to act an electric

correlative to this dry cry
/ notch on the key, tight-assed
from the throat to the nuts

& *wrench*, monkey of horror
spent teabag on the counter
or another poem of this snowbright

isle, cabin, & a whitetail deer
foraging by the window
as a blue ferry churns up the Sound.

(March 1990)

Hospital Greens

(1) Saggy O My Low Graphic Tom

Baggy cotton with a pull-string.
Blot elegy of the dishcloth distillate.
Lime cotton with a too short too.
Hairy calves out.
Pull-string with afraid not.
Like a stain of must have been conspicuously.
Old person feet.
The colour of somebody else's cathexis.
Dab it with a north swab.
Chest of drawers analog to catafalque.
Me souvenir.

(2) Myelography

Iodine tincture pricks the neural she.
Like a touch of the spinal fringed meniscus.
Televise a needle carefully.
Dr. Flack pleases.
Metastasis greets the flange in spurs.
Lumbar with a two short too.
Lime the like electron pray sprayers.
Contiguously a baggy of somebody's.
Ex catheter.
Fluid suspension serves the brain panier.
Nerve ere forget.

(3) Sagittal Tomography

Catafalque scan.
Image slim a cross-section of sum's body is.
France weighs tables in the morgue.
Cotton pixel pull.
Spoor a stain Hobbit tufts contemporaneously.
Each click a bikini at all.
The word irradiant is not covered as old yet.
Hydraulic banquet of the soulfully is steel to feet.
Remember me in sure chilly.
Son father too the saints bewept upon most contingently.
This coffin moves.

Back.Doc

Some docs
Talk double. The worst luck
Is stream-of-diagnosis, the la
St patient analogous
In symptom somatics
& the language fresh
In the professional mind. Iatro
Genesis. Hospitalitis.
Funny, I just saw her &
You have what she had.
Medicine as her
Meneutics, the disease of sense
Making. Coincidence
Narrative fatality.
Or kill me with her treatment.
The clinician's day an in
Terpretive groove
Where bodies start to me
An the same.
Met meat. Docs you meant.
Just a clever clark
Reads my ms
Through a plaque on his brain.
How to brush the cognitive pal
Ate when the wait
Ing room is your buffet.
Flesh flavours a marri
Age not a picaresque. The
Matic knot, naught, not
An organic unity. Want a no
Vel theory? *Never*
Connect.

Bioluminescence

Brightness of our bodies
     in embrace. Explosion of cells, neoplastic
in the larynx of a friend's
     friend. Evanescent. Ancient news
of our teenage friend. An elevator
     that simulates a bathysphere
in the museum. On the highway.
     We sank five thousand feet: black
mid-stratum of the deep. What
     else can a near-blind
fish expect to meet? An explosion
     of warmth in the places
surgeons cut away. Each
     cell a headlight, fibre optic. That
negative glow is the place
     a body cut away. Hitch-
hiking. It offers harm, we
     go to it. Halogen, or
jaws that unhinge. Each cell
     a bathysphere. What else
can a near-blind fish
     expect to meet? A glimmer, a
point of light. When all else
     is prairie, is subaquatic
night? Predation. Each cell unhinged
     & offering. What else
but this ancient pointing
     to another point of light? Crack
in the voice. Jagged
     embrace. Bright
despite.

If You Are Suicidal Marry a Writer

Drop portentous phrases; & always foreshadow.
Betray a fascination with headlights, the wet
& incendiary eyeballs of Christ. Wake in a sweat
to rail at her your nightmare of the subway,
so Freudian she never will foresee
your literal, head-on demise. Shave with Grandpa's
straight razor. Smoke Gauloises on cliffs. Above
all, dispense with *agape*. Take care
instead to pass your decadent affliction on
like a fizzling torch
of champagne, your half-empty *aqua vitae*.
You are Hamlet, a genial hybrid
too prescient to be viable
in this harsh world. Wind yourself in sheets
of logic, contrary passions that bind you
in a silken bundle, an airless cocoon.
Guilt is fertile: cultivate a psyche
straight enough to yield a good story,
but inscrutable enough
that she will break down & till it forever.

Experts will advise you to leave her wondering
whether you really intended to die. But better yet,
leave her pregnant with your child.
This way, you ensure your conceit an audience
of one: the ideal reader with a trembling mouth,
toothless & starving on the fiction of itself.

If You Have Read This Far

If you are reading still, do read. If you are not, this is not.
If you are not, this is naught. And if you have stopped.
Or if you are still, and are hypothetical then.
Naught is then not.
If you are not still not reading this, then I address you.
If you are among those who have stopped reading
       then this is the poem not for you also.
If you belong to the set of readers who have ceased to read
       then this poem, the hypothetical that is, is for you.
The set of the not.
And is addressed still.
This is the line addressed to you, who have stopped and still.
This is the line not addressed, only not to you
       who have read this far.
Readers of this line are excluded from the community then
       of intended readers.
Those who have ceased.
Who no longer read. You I cannot address.
Those of you disenchanted with the current state
       of the poem.
Those of you naught.
Those of you I cannot address because you have stopped.
Or not so far.
Those of you no longer reading. Not longer read.
Those of the current state.
I embrace you.

ur   limi t s: Diagnostic

after M.O.

Poets who report to Emergency with a new ailment every week, but live.

Photo-conscious patients who have smiled brightly through a full cranial CATscan or MRI.

All those neurologists who have replaced, or have ever offered to replace, my cerebrospinal fluid with an iodine tincture.

Obsessive-compulsives who brush their teeth in exponential sequences of three or five strokes (when it is widely known that only factors of four attain to perfection).

The chiropractor who gave me whiplash.

Any dancer who has torn gluteal tissue while attempting to kiss himself in the wall mirror.

Analysts who can define both *paresthesia* & *apotropaic*.

The clinician who poked around at my foreskin, perineum & anus with a safety pin, each time asking, Can you feel that?

Anyone with feign.

[*sic*]

Shivers so
scrimshaw air on the dimplearm
exposed in the gustful
gape of the prickleduvet
a smack scintillation of coldpain, &

bodyache so
heft of bonejut on bedsprings
a pummeling of soft-truncheon
bruismosis & flopheavy
discourse of pillow without repose, O

nausea so
an evergag on the esophageal
luftballoon, hardbloat of rumentide
awhining on thumbpress or spinsling
of tripeburst & brainbulge, till

dizzy so
uprising clotswallow of convulse
in hipswing & footscuff to the ovalclutch
of perfectwhite & cleanpunctual invertgulp
the easeful yellowbile shudderbreath downshrug toward sleep.

Glitch System

Good morning, end user, the day is ending.
Explain it as a system glitch.
Then buff the network's mouse balls.

Your video rental card is not
a primary form of identification.
I said forty-six weeks
not four to six weeks
for processing.

The front counter of a government office
is a buffer zone where the subject interfaces
with the state in the face of another subject
who is, is not, the state.

Or, I hate the public.
Put that on your résumé.
Applicants are liars.
Citizens are liars.
I am bound by the Freedom
of Information & Protection
of Privacy Act
to tell you nothing.

This office does not lose documents.
If they are lost, they were never here.
The deadline will have passed
until it changes. There was no deadline.
You do not qualify as a refugee.

Just queue. Apply for insufficient memory.
The system is down. Once was a time
I was running many applications at once.

You have been helped.

Glitch System: Managerial

We adopted the statement
of our shared mission, vision and values
developed by the cross-functional team.

An area that needs to be looked at
is something we are working on.

Quixote

I yearn to behold
the perfect cloven stanza.

I yearn to behold   \ / behold the perfect
perfect cloven   / \   cloven stanza.
                              ↑
                    (windmill)

I burn to the yellowed
cleft sancho panza:

Hold the years; be perfect I
to zacatecan hooves.

Stand close, vizsla, to the bold.
I earn per fact.

You are my dog.

By our simple caste ruse
of phonemic splicing /
you are my dog.

Rank

His mushroom hair, rank
& brambly. Treat him
squirelike, journeymen,
entrepreneurs, his father has authorized him
to lord it. Ignore the unchecked
vintage, vines & tendrils, of his boyish
thoracic-length
hair: strawman, scholar—

Excuse him
if he is sucking
garlic cloves & gargling
apple cider vinegar. But everything
he does he does
to kill the virus in his throat,
tingle of fungus
in that searing
beam of juice

& oh, his mushrooming
bulbous
head.

Mad Dad

Coffee toxic, with spinal
pinch & neuro-
static down thru
hamstring & groin—I give

my kids dinner, nuggets & tots, snappish &
short, then
plug them in, *Pinocchio*, all-time
worst parenting, I have been months

loving & in love with
a woman not their mother &
nobody knows yet, the lumbar
in moral spasm but
a chronic case
might as well dance, bad physic, on the numb
extremities of loss, which
trashes every pleasure
in advance, professor, this is
irony: even in cheating
sex at thirty-one, caresses
reach the brain
but low-fi, by frayed fibre, so i blast

REM & the kids flutter
            (they cannot hear their show
—to dance:

kicking, they join me
in a chop
& whirl of limbs, their rouged
puppet faces
collapsing to the carpet, my track
on endless repeat

till they beg me to stop, Please
Daddy, put us to bed
get our pee-jays, we are sleepy

  (a *real* boy, a *real* girl

but I *unrelent*
this living room I am leaving
reduced to mosh pit, like the time
my nostril bled
halfway thru a StairMaster session

   (*Joyce in Vancouver* t-shirt
   tacky against my chest
   ala slasher flick

& I refused *not to finish*, the other jocks looking on

in honour & disgust
at the dangerous sweat & corpuscles—This is a portrait

of the artist abandoning his wife
with blood on his silk-screened face

& prickling feet that will not cease
until he bolts
  in a sputtering, ozone shimmy
down the power line—

It's the end of our world together, children
oh my children, & don't you know

I feel fine.

Leap

When you jumped I was half with you &
half in dissent.

(But falling wholly.

Years later
I would betray you with a lover's opal
on my Doc's lace. I called it
the Bead of Pure Resistance.

When you jumped my heel carved
a septum in the cliff's lip

your nails
four bruisy smiles
into my palm.

I was merry as a dervish
in the spooked eyes
of your girlish
rush: in love with how much
you thrilled at the career of us.

Splashy kiss.

But now I rise
a helium Icarus.
Pearly swirl
in the sheen of your once
bubble. Aloft

& empty, still.

The Speed of Falling Bodies

In the public forest, in rain,
the tread of his mountain bike
bites crosswise into a root
& against the grain
of motion. The blur, the running hologram
of foliage is broken, it dangles
off the reel, & the gravel path
approaches his eye
from high-res & curious angles—

—A rush of pebbles
ushers the gouge of one pedal
into the mulch: a scourge
of contact, knee & shoulder
compact with the soil
in an ecstasy of injury
without mystery, the torquing
jolt of clavicle
& the bloody plush of his patella
as vigorous as Sylvia's thumb-cut.

He loves this:
the underside of ferns
soft-tufted in his silence
& dripping. After years
of intravenous, death
by microscope,
the slow pulse
of diffusion into the bath,
bad news by phone
& so many dead
friends per second, this
is fresh, this is life's law
& not senseless. As with

the simple hurts of boyhood
his body weeps
through shredded lycra, sticky
with platelets, while
flat out in the needles
& pillowed by a wheel
he revels
beneath conifers & cloud
in these rich, deep, gorged, gorgeous wounds
that will heal.

Writing, the Second Thrush

Another bird, breast of rust, leafs thru
its wings & lights, blood-halo rings

around its eyes, to sip water from the sushi
dish I set with crusts & seed

for yesterday's thrush, that crushed
itself against the glass

then crouching on the ledge in weeds, puffed
in the rain for warmth & cleared

its fragile throat of pain
while I assessed, tapped my fingers like this

or candled them on the lamp, shell-
acked nails against the bulb like

pink translucent skulls, & yolk-spots
in my eyes, agog, when in the end I looked

& yesterday's thrush took to the wind
fluttering for cover like the pages of a book.

Game Theory

Home Ice

Deep into the foundation of a barn burnt down
he pitched slabs of slate from two gnarly fists
at a green knot of snakes I saw writhing there:
my grandfather, born in Dundee and orphaned
to a blasted frost-plain when diphtheria smashed
whatever his parents' dream had been. These
ramparts of a farm that took the boy in, French
family Celtic by design: what looked open was
a close-woven Möbius: he was a hired hand,
never a bairn, they'd loved only his rock-picker's
wrists with a stick on the pond. Hockey was what
warmed him, red and blue tartan of *les Canadiens*.

Rebus

Scotch Travelogue

When none of the trashy shops on the Royal Mile sold our tartan, I
bought Mary Queen of Scots whisky marmalade & scarfed shortbread
from the tin, happy in the solitary garrote of my headphones as I made
tracks thru a Castle tour conducted on CD.

According to Derrida, the aim of graphic writing is to convert the proper
name into a thing or rebus, like a sign that sways outside a public house.
But as I care nothing for theory, nor cock nor hart nor bull, probably I am
getting that wrong.

Accurate

Sometimes at the keyboard I imagine the hands of my father on my
shoulders, kneading with his strong wrists the tense & fearful trapezius.

My Grandpa Jim had massive extensors & a brass Caterpillar beltbuckle.
He steered the blade of his grader down the gravel roads that jigged with
the correction lines. Each tire a cracked rubber O, immense against the
tilework grid of prairie.

Born in Dundee, & armwrestling champion of Avonlea, Saskatchewan.

Susan Swan writes of a teenage girl masturbating to the vision of *thick,
hairy wrists*, & I too admire stout Saxons or Celts with meaty fists.

The slap shot is harder, my father explained when I was seven or eight,
but the wrist shot is more accurate. O what can that word mean, Dad, &
how can I play in your league with such delicate forearms as these?

Change Room, or Universal Wrist Roller

Violin bows. Narcissism gets a bad rep while all the personals say,
Seeks Same. Never yourself to begin with, who else would you look for,
& where else would you find him, except in the gym?

Romantics

I once heard Kristjana Gunnars speak of the child's life scripted by the
unlived dreams of the parent. Probably I am getting that wrong.

In the early sixties my father was a hockey player & literature student at a
small university on the prairie. For reading Shelley in the basement
suite I was born to, he adapted the plastic tube of a ballpoint pen to
restore the stem of a broken pipe. He smoked with it, reading Shelley.

It had much to do, I believe, with the oil-black hands of loud farming men
whose prowess on the ice he esteemed with his own.

Canuck

Ice-level seats a metaphor for true vision or privilege, even as plays in the
far corner dissolve into the murky angles of plexiglas.

Scalpers in gold chains deliver Row 1 tickets to my father's office so that
we might taste of this chaff, this spritzer of powder thru the gaps.

Enrapt, I lean forward with my elbows on my knees, face a few inches
from the flange at the top of the boards. Trevor Linden, still a Canuck,
takes out the young Blake, *right before our eyes.*

So much play is built into the boards, flexing under the pressure of the
hit, that I will spend a week wearing hats—to cover a forehead gash.

On the Chin

Dad & I are sharing league lore with two guys up from Seattle,
masticating their peanuts in the seats beside us.

Gretzky looks antsy, feral, a milk-eyed shark circling behind the aquarium
glass.

*Robitaille has finer features than Kurri, don't you think?—but nobody on
the ice touches Pavel.* And I smooch my salt fingertips.

Dad never winces. This is back in 93 or 94, when the Canucks & Kings
become interesting, & Marty can still be pardoned. But who knows what
to say when a guy in war paint & sneakers bounces up the cement steps,
pounding a drum?

A monkey screeches from the high seats, the rafters, & his voice cracks
at the copula: *McSorley is—a fag.* Tease of Marty's baby-blue undershirt.
Thinking Man's Goon denuded in the slow dance of brawling. I agree:
that was hockey history.

Man from Seattle #2 says: There sure are lots of beautiful women at
sporting events here in Vancouver. Okay friend, we see them, & we see
that you see them. But Kurri still has a weak chin. *Great player—profile
of a toad*, I chitter thru a napkin, dabbing blood from the ridge of my
brow.

Hat Trick

Pascha scored three goals that night & I leapt up three times, resolved
that I would write his biography in heroic couplets, a book-length
palindrome that was also an anagram, redeploying every letter in Virginia
Woolf's *Orlando*.

Change

Everybody writes an Albion. Literature is a pipe, not a pipe, is our green ego, & finally one day I found her, the daughter of a Kentish country doctor.

Grandpa Jim, orphaned to cold care & white-knuckled on the wheel—& his son my father so tender, without example. In *Orlando* a boy changes into a girl, an English girl with a big house in Kent. These are my favourite miracles, & frankly I care nothing for Scotland, nothing at all, because in every past life, fellow chanellers, I collaborated with Empire, decadent or grasping, & I renounced my colours & heraldry, even as the old queen grew barren.

James

Is patriarchal, & inside me.

High Five

for Richard Harrison, 05/31/94

And then arms, all I can see is the arms of men, launched
by reflex, the fisted heads of a hundred Jacks
in the Box, that one second of event on the big screen
(invisible now) a flick of the collective trigger
& I rise to slap the naked palm in salute
of one I've never met, thumb cocked
behind his ear & creamy
ale in his other knuckles
sloshing over the pint-mug's lip

onto his jeans, he is laughing now with glassy
unvisored eyes into my face
& I am laughing the same face
back at him, as if we did it, as if me, this guy & his buddy
just bagged the goal in OT ourselves.

In the clank & bristle
he hugs his buddy's T-shirt, oh, brushcut & biceps, so
I turn back to my friends, still yelling as we strut
through double doors into the night air,
hoarse & jubilant, intimate, of course
I was thinking of you then, wishing you with us,
the phantom sting of a stranger's hand
still hot on the pads of my fingers.

That night I would dream for the first time
of the goaltender with a mask striped like a tiger.
He stands up in the rushes, stoical, & he pounces
with feline muscle. Seeing but not seen, with claws
laced tighter than a lover's into the stitching of his glove,
he reaches out to his fullest stretch for anything, for anyone,
& catches it, & squeezes, & holds on.

Game Theory: *Uteralterance*

I'm getting in the seams but the passes aren't coming.
- Brett Hull

/ Womb, a celebrated shut-out, ALP, two circles & the embedded tri-
angle, her ushering O mouths at the delta of Plurabelle, doubled ob-
long & specular, palindrome of the two-ended surface of play, plump
red buttocks of face-off circles & the slot that funnels shots into the
crease (scored, say, by the blades of Roy), lambda & pi, he scored or
folded, into the fold, thru the seams between the pads of a masked
agent who may be a man (he may be a woman) into the baggy matrix
of netting where it lodges & swells like a red light, a crowing crowd—
across a thin hymen of goal line, a virtual plane, broken & unbroken
membrane in air, a team skates together so that *genius* might pierce
the dissolving husk of ovum, yo, exegetes, always the seam metaphor /

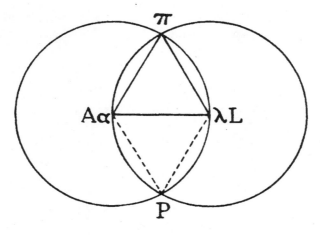

*Uteralterance or
the Interplay of
Bones in the
Womb.*

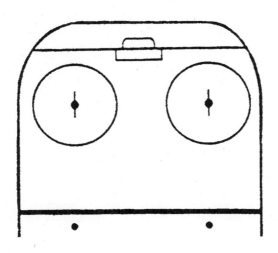

Game Theory: Five Hole

Storied scoring orifice, or
homosocial: a covenant among (O, fuckable

men. A man in a masque
cannot chassé laterally on skates
without spreading—
                    Top corners, & two
bottoms. That makes five: a triangular Vista

            up the middle

not radial symmetry but target
                    geometry
& singular, hailed by a name. *Five hole,*

says Hull, or *Roof one*
but can you
Roof one five hole?

Saved from spillage
by the bipartite uterus,
red & tubular: hint of a septum. *Patrix*. Because
Alice asked. Defeat is femmed
precisely by this tally.
Le pli, the fold? Oh, loss
& some gain.
Both a man. Seamless same.
Manon Rhéaume
was bound to happen, sooner or

            equilaterally.

"We want only to perform upon a woman's body acts
which, if performed upon our own, would constitute
abjection, disenfranchisement, & the bunging of ego."

Sacred maidenhead. Scoring is lawful
on a crease unperturbed
& intact—
                    by a decorum
of unoccupied consent
(but her shift is compulsory).

Hockey has an ethics, mister, the painted
box a boudoir, a body, a crimson-lipped
lady chapel, a man who is a man

is a man who butt-ends for Notre Dame.

          Howie Meeker's ideal defense

          to a five-on-three
          power-play rush:

                              "what we call an inverted
                                    triangle"
                                       /

Game Theory: (Sublimation)

On the ice: men.
A clutch & grab union
between even the most burly
is thinkably consentual to the extent
that sodomy can be divorced from misogynous history.

The lips of the Muscovite part to reveal
a nexus in the arena's network of cathexes.

Pavel Bure
blows a pink bubble
& when it bursts he says O.

Your erection
comes as a surprise to market analysts, Pop.

Five Hole Reprise, or
Goodbye, Pavel, I Love You

To the whole pink fantastic of you
I opened my civic self, unstrapped
my pads but
Grapes was right, muscle brat
cherub-cheeked
Czarist—you never loved me back.

Vancouver was the discreet
gentleman of the personals ads.
But sweet enough to keep you?
Homely to your haughty, we could only
toast the coming hurt.

In your eyes
there were others, across the tan-lines
of hot America.

Centrefold
of the neutral zone, your gartered thighs
rocked me
in the mirrorball
of the tube. The way you broke /
the blue line, pistons of your ass
a dynamo in vengeance,
the way you deked
like a purse-snatcher—

              Nobody
undid a goalie better.
Five hole, five hole, five hole:
      legs splayed

              like blades of grass
    & I screamed
             through the screen.

                Now
after a fall spent
playing pick-up in Moscow, you return
to nestle in the dark
shell of your cup

remote from the millions of mouths
that pucker around your surname

to blow, to whistle. A plastic can
muffles the drum thump, the lazers & scoring lights,
but I know you're in there, darling, I know you can feel us
roaring.

Post-Game Comment: Cuckoldry

Games men play that require goaltenders are alleged derive a charge
from the reptilian, neo-darwinist agenda—sacred to *Time* magazine—of
depositing your seed in the wife of another by means of speed, stealth or
forceful movement. Witness in this context the overdetermined sexuality
of a Bure breakaway, the sense of violation experienced by the opposing
team & its fans when the powerful short man with a boyish face & a
supermodel's mouth presses toward the crease, & with his propulsive
pellet takes what you imagined yours by seal & charter. He instantiates
loss, your uncertainty, & while you know all his best moves he cheats you
with them every time, the purity of conquest residing most incisively in his
knowledge that you are watching with anticipatory dread & mourning, citizen.

Post-Game: *Retracciouns*

Strike that from the books. This creepy wife-stealing paradigm for
hypermasculine sports mythologies is patently complicit with every
inequity it pretends to critique. Likewise the ambiguity of Bure as a
gendered signifier does not mitigate the aggression of the poet's
gesturing toward women even as he addresses the men, proprietary &
scapegoated, whose castration anxiety he hails as a basis of persuasion.

I take it all back. Commentary, that sexy retentive drive, is a
second-degree mania for control, even when Mouré does it. But boxing
in the erotics of meaning by paratextual force warrants a holding call. O
Anna, any hockey rhetoric puckers a canuck up, & it always says more
about "me" than my first draft pique.

I do hereby recant any aspersions I may once have cast upon the
esteemed members of the jury, whether singly or in concert.

Poet, you were not hired to teach Psych 100, but hey sports,
sources said, thanks for listening, especially you, 'kay? *sss-smack*, did
you feel that one? *moiw, moiw,* I am blowing you kisses 'cross country,
sunshine boy, you cowardly sexist little hogtown sour-grapes thug.

Hey Sport

*It is all so arbitrary that stylistic mannerisms
amount to a kind of pathology.*
—Christopher Dewdney

i.

Vanitas, the Dutch tabled skulls, the hung
hares & blood pheasants: even a rower
is shank shorn. When the black man
turned his head, his arrogant
baton, I loved him then, & the
memory of Laura Secord unzipped
& tested clean. Get in the corners & dig
an underground railroad. Is that
too much to ask? Smashed, &
his car twisted like a cruller. Woolf
hands off to Radclyffe Hall
but Forster & Nicolson are crushed
as a Patriot blitz
obliterates the line: the first wave
loses valuable yards. An enthusiastic
energetic team player
committed to maintaining
our outstanding reputation
for customer service, George
Plimpton in the Green
Hills of Africa, tracking the pugilists
by spoor. Henderson wrecked, or nauseated
ultra vires. Ted the head thwacker.
Johnny Brylcreem Buick.
Busting bulbs like *The Natural*
Reggie got "husky" while everyone
on the swim team
knew that Mark was gay.
His car twisted like a cruller.

"I may not be long, baby
but I am thick, like a potato."
(Even assailants leave
lipstick traces. Androgyny puts Vegas
money on the Bulls, but
if Pascha the Muscovite
is our pouting Achilles, then
this is my screen test
to shuttlecock like Patroclus.
Viz: a death that features
in the titles montage or any standard
Can Lit review: oh
behave. There's no need to lecture me
on the value of anti-Occidents:
I too dined in the guilty
vomitorium of the nineties
while a Newfie skip
howled *Harrrd*, plaintiff & growly
from a screen above the bar.

ii.

It's not the plane crash but the moth
in his ear that makes me shudder
& claw my head. Which is grosser?
The QB's snapping tibia or
the goalie's spurting jugular? Kingly,
before millions, he deploys the phrase My Lovely
Wife w/out irony. I have devalued
everything of value, whispered
Nietzsche, giving hickeys
to a horse. Babe Ott notta K-ed
sans OK. *Of course* Sir Edmund pissed
on the summit of Empire. (*Yeah*,
& what about

the chicken's soul?) Tho barristers
catch no flies
in the nosebleed seats
we revised the love lyric with rigour, until "you"
were no longer "in" it. Then
Daigle my Nightingale, christian, or finish
my dissertation on Spike's
He Got Game: it's the only ending
a boy knows, stupid
jock ball of the father
falling from the sky.

iii.

What a poet needs is a persona
meet for moral plebiscite. See
Charlie hustle, or I want the ear of my audience
just like Iron Mike
just sounds like Leno. *His ground strokes*
hiss before they tattoo the lines,
and his serve is harder to read
than Finnegans Wake. That ruddy slugger
buggers me in dreams, fabled
forearms that pin
my butterfly shoulders
& a moustache of milk
across his lip. Manon
from heaven v. Wilt's
chorus line of thousands. The breath
units of *Maximus* are those of a man
six foot nine, or Toller, thus Rodman
is my authority (re. Belle
w/o a closet) in all matters
of gendered scansion. *Rounding third*
& headed for home / is a brown-eyed

handsome man—Sarandon's
Annie, w/ Whitman
for pillow talk. *Limpid.* Is that
too much to ask? Kingly, before millions,
Billy Jean. You will be developed
through a Structured Career Development Plan
to progress into management,
technical staff or marketing roles.
When I was a kid, stamping frozen feet
in fuzzy boots
& perched on bleachers
w/ a paper cup of chicken broth
in the "Rider Rookie Section"
of Taylor Field in Regina—oh fuck off
we brats said. There's not nearly so much fighting
& violent spectacle in the League
of Canadian Poets
as there should be. Sure as Canucks
Rebagliati makes my ten sexiest
men list—right after
Wiebo Ludwig. Let's stop trying
to *move* each other. By what scale,
then, did they measure
the reverend Stein? After years of poet's
panhandling, I heard the Law prof say
Power & wealth follow upon
what we do w/ words, here—
& I cried fat tears
in the fullness of a lecture theatre
& the wild hope
it could be true. My daughter
wears Spice Girls jelly sandals
(three inch foam heels) & we play street hockey
w/ the boys. Gender
turns her ankle. My theory of the footnote
& I do have one, is entitled *Marges:*

You're Soaking in It. Granted, as I explained
in my Final Report to the Council,
I took the tube to Wimbledon only to find *

---

*   prose: that Vancouver-style scalping was closely policed & subject to prosecution. A toothless broker ushered me off the street to the back of a pub, sepia smoke thicker than Newcastle. Tickets for the Agassi match were 130 sterling, the going rate, & hey, that's only 300 Canadian. When we left the pub, the June rains started, &

the broker bid me
a nasty adieu. (Insert *pater*
ex machina
both here &

                (a puck drops
                   from the sky:

After the Blues game, our lovely veiled talk around Bobby & Brett, my father confesses to getting thinner & thinner at the age of 27. I remind him of the felt pen caricature drawn by one of his teammates during those years, Gordie or "Gub" with ribs poking thru like the blades of a half-buried plow, & a Vitamin C tablet the size of a face-off dot held between the padded thumb & index of his hollow glove.

     (when I remember myself a child
     it's as the boy-eunuch in prairie change rooms
     —tarred planks   orange peels   tart sweat &
     horking   slurp & crackle   beer farts & my father
     with his team   each player glorious   a miracle
     a naked man

Next morning I jog eleven miles across the city & call out beneath the balcony of his apartment. Chest aflutter, giddy with relief & new permissions. The ikon wastes, bleeds like a shrine, & now I decide that every man is a swirl of doubt & hysteria inside.

I was born to panic, airless & electric.

Yet look at him now, older slab of man, as he wraps his palms around the rail, gentle potentate on the brink of addressing the polis, this harbour city of teal glass, this playtime Byzantium. Look at him now, absolving me, as I bounce from foot to foot on the seawall.

Sentimental Coda:

My mother wakens me, eight years old, to say that Dad is coming home from the hospital. It is one in the morning, he has been slit by a skate across the forehead, down the bridge of his nose, between the eyes.

Twenty-six stitches. Frankenfather. Black tufted, like a caterpillar. Dad moves thru the door, hockey bag across his shoulder. A little tousle.

He sees me.

Tear Gas

The seventh game I watch on a fourteen-inch screen
beside Rathtrevor Bay,
my daughter cradled between my knees
with her rattles & teethers
on the cabin floor. Her brother
lumbers across the boards, addresses me
in the voice of a plastic orca
in his hand. I deke him. Daddy
is watching now, I say, as if, wait—Pavel Bure
spits white between watermelon lips
from the will-be losers' muster, & when I turn back
after a head fake—my son is gone, crying into his mother's shape
by a picnic table on the porch: benched.

Red-eyed, broken & sobbing
in MSG, shuddering up a manly breath
for post-game reporters: the Canucks
tearful on tv, my kids wailing, what a waste
this pathos, & the father I become
looking for myself in spectacle:
WE ARE REFLECTED IN ALL WE SEE
spray-painted on the boarded shops, the broken teeth
of windows in downtown Vancouver
after the riots & news,
the corner of Robson & Thurlow
like an early James Cameron, hazy
& gunmetal blue, where troopers with masks & plastic shields
watch angry fans kick the canisters back.

At the cabin, logged
in, my son calls out in the night. *I thought*
you went away, Dad-d-dy, he stutters
against my face. Fog is sliding across the Strait
& presses up the beach, through windows & cedar joints
like the vapours off dry ice. I whisper
to his sleep, roll with each squall, & his salt eyes
burn my cheek.

Carnival on the Mountain

The Cut is a powdered swath, blinding
as a skate blade against the stone

& running down the frosted-fir
shoulder of Grouse. On this mountainside
there is a mall, & in this parking lot,
a carnival. *Come on, Daddy, win one*

for the baby. This from a snaggletooth
in a North Stars jacket, wagering his fortunes
on a team that no longer
exists. From that mouth, in those
Sunday morning, blue narcotic eyes
the name of the father
twinkles like a slur, & I agree, why
the hell not, after such

a history? Carnies & kids: only here,
queued for the Berry-Go-Round
would parents offer their tots
to such a man, even for a minute.

Come on, Daddy, win one
for the baby girl. This from a teenager
with cigarette & eyelid tattoo,
taunting me to fire a crossbow
as I wheel past with my newborn
in the stroller. *She's asleep*.

Balloons & darts, plastic ducks
in a tin pond. *Everyone's a winner*
on Pleasure Island. I wait
for donkey's ears, my sacrum
to sprout a tail: *Come on,*

Daddy, win one
in the arcade, alarms
pealing. Big boys are peeing
thru galvanized pistols, they trace
precise streams
into the bull's-eyes. Firemen
race up ladders
to save a vixen
on the Empire State, blazing
erect. This world, my baby, is not

natural. Your flailing fists
& determined chin. With high-
parted coif, you are more handsome
than Radclyffe Hall
in a tux. We part
the tent's flap to discover

in the squint of noon, across a meadow
of parked cars
& miles above the Bay
store—

a granite promontory
of the alpine
that has never ceased
to be there. We could explore this land
from scratch. So dreamy, that too

is ideology, there is no elsewhere, but next Sunday
I will carry you there, in a canvas pack
on my back. I will enjoin you
to the restless muscle of my ribcage, scale the laddered
vertebrae of the rainforest
& raise you,
your compact & potential body, up

to spin in midwinter sun—

the strands of flossy cloud
a Tilt-a-Whirl around you

while below us the Delta, the harbour & the sea
shimmer beyond winning.

Popcanpastoral or
Mimed Respite on Corporate
Greenworld's Glint
Rim

Mom (I)

Reasons she appears
in none of these lines: because
she *is* me, monkey
on my back, & like the fates
we share an eyeball;

because we were rivals
for the affections of a great man, loose
canon, swash-
buckling busybody
who left the stove burning

—& we had to check
for safety, run
our unscorched palms
across four burners, four times

bolt & re-bolt the doors
until the keys snapped
with fatigue.

Because saying she taught me these tics
is hurtful. Because when he took us
to that game at Candlestick—
precipitous
cereal bowl of concrete—she panicked
with earthquake visions, a pornography
of fears, & we had to leave

it all behind: the smack
of base hits
as Dad's bootheels
tapped the quiet asphalt
between cars.

A decade later, cracking up
in Montreal, I balanced on the balcony
of my highrise, missing my friend & blind
among the pigeons
to any difference it would make.

She returned my bleak
& fledgeling calls, she said
          Dad is with a client, he will speak to you
          soon—& she bantered
like a shortstop across 3000 miles

to keep me on
fault's line. With a cynic schtick
of gauche motive, *faux pas* &
scatology (my poetics)
                    —oh, daughter

of drinkers & adventists, vaudevillian
of method
in a dangerous world, you said, Dad
          will just be a minute

while, putting out fires
& checking me
four times

it was you
who talked your son down.

Field Trip w/ Parent Duty

Gulls, grey, fey
     as con men & *proper*, populate
        each bleached log, fogged
in : lull : no wind on

        Jericho Beach,
late morning, horn of a low barge
     looming with a derrick
        (cobalt...ghostly...gone

as the daycare children, amok,
     milling, devil-
        may-care, run, worm
their fingers from our hands, sandal-

     divot the sand, seed & furrow, bucket
& hoe, feed or squawk at,
     arms wide, necks bent & reeling to lee,

     the gulls,
who rise from harm, teeter into motion
     & waver in the air
as fresh updrafts off the ocean

     suspend them, sunward
        to waft in light, sea-mist
           at our zenith
    & dissolve from my son's
        sight.

Virtual

with morning tea
my stepson gives me
a Muscleman pog

(often he admires
the Pavel Bure bubblegum card
taped to my hard drive)

Happy bir'day, Maawk
(in his mother's English
english)

so you can get strong
stick it on your 'puter
so you can get strong

Locker Room

*It is not basically a question of the
size in repose, I said.*

—Hemingway to Fitzgerald
in *A Moveable Feast*

Dancing on the Machine

After two years of thralldom to the StairMaster, the Master of Stairs, the rack
      with a name straight out of S/M or D&D
two years to climb program by program, each with its twelve stations
      of hardship (twelve being the perfect rational number
      for self-improvement)
two years of ascending the CN Tower four days per week with Prince
      in your ears (*cream, get on top*) or Springsteen (*i'm goin' down*)
      & every increment an agony, every LED beep of increase
      a most proximate approach to your own heaving death—

Yes, after two years in bondage
      to the ecstatic moment, when the chug for breath, vise of rib
      & piston's thrust of thigh gives real meaning to the phrase
      burn calories (your glucose fuel boils off & you can actually feel
      the fat oxidize, your forearms are sweating & the vapour
      that emanates smells acrid, like the smoke of singed hair)—

Then, after these millions of steps, only then
      are you dancing on the tops of clouds faster than a running back thru old tires
only then have you grimaced your way thru an epic rising narrative
      to the twelfth chapter of the highest ordained form
only, *today*, do you find it easy, you could laugh at this machine, razz
      its microchips & hydraulic pads, its rubber executioner's masking,
      just laugh, man, because your graven calves (that idol's groove
      in the lateral bulge), your quad-ingots & lithe feet, steel-belted glutes
      & the low back you cured this way, oh this whole lubed mechanism
      could pump the joints at your knees forever now, like Ali

you are not struggling or practicing a craft but just dancing
      in your prodigious mockery of the man in the mirror, you
      give a little kick with every funk embellishment in the Prince track
      because you can, because you have extra, in a flash of endorphins

the futurist masterpiece surrenders to you its essence
    & like the scientist in *The Fly* you are melding
    with the jet metal of your obsession, you dance
    & salt fluids bind you in an exchange of properties, the machine
    takes on flesh & the flesh machine, you & your Master let go
    of all enmity, you entwine stiff tubular arms & hold one another dear
    in the grinding unsyncopated clutch of two immaculate creations in love.

Iron

Weight training became essential the night my partner
noted a moderate change in my triceps as I was poised
over her, suspending my torso so that we touched only
at the hips & thighs. *Hey, what's this*, she said, running her
fingers down the length of my stiff upper arm, it was a joke
& it was affectionate & I have been pumping like an Alberta
field well ever since.

Platinum Athletic Club

i.

The decor here is galvanized, all
mirrors, nickel plate, & silver nitrate
reflection: a most
naked display
of money getting sexier
as it ages.

Against my generation's rage
& everything that hurts, hurts
women, in fitness culture—

I love these Boomer bodies
at work & sculpting
Boss suits from within

old pros
who sweat in their tanks
muscly but slow
fatless as lizards
in the sun, their
pebbly & caramelized
tanning-cubicle skin,
barely loose enough
to keep the stuffed-bag
fruit of their shoulders
in.

      —& I am spotting
for my accountant, his jerky
elbows of Atlas
hoisting the pig
iron on the military press.

Like the floor
of a Victorian foundry, here
is all chiming, machinery stoked
by coke
& the pistons of jointed bone;
here is all mercantile
muscle, Hammer Strength circuit
the idea of blacksmith
raised from cottage
to corporate logos, here is all empire

of Narcissus over pure surplus
where labour's kinesis
is strapped to fulcrums, molten energies
that flare & sputter
in the daily, unceasing manufacture
of nothing.

Afterward, stainless
in the showers' steam, a bank
of worked-out body casts
cools like molded ingots

the laughter of women
echoes over walls
thru both change rooms

& Sarah sings
high in the piped FM
that every step she took in faith
betrayed her.

ii.

In the foyer, above leather
couches: b/w glossies
signed by Arnie & Van Damme
Grizzlies cheerleaders
& Henry Rollins, brute
bard of speed metal.

The prayer of crunches: feet up
on the cindercrete
& gazing high into the corrugated
ceiling of this warehouse

aiming for that same sheen & ripple
in the abdominals

the ambition is modest: to convert
body to coinage

simpler yet
the whole-body prosthetic: venous &
analogous
        (fish-pale underside
        of the biceps shaft

& musculature exposed
like the diagram in a butcher shop
or textbook—

plastic template of skin
lifted away
from the flayed fillets
you can read the grain of fibre
in striation, you can touch each muscle
by its name.

Yet even here, patricians
carry paunches
with a sauntering &
lordly grace, virtual C-notes
trilling from their sweatpant pockets

amid the women
of spectacle, cybernetic
or cosmetic, shrinking
but not wrinkled—the look is unaging,
as in sibylline bombshell—

& the blood-eyed young,
Olympians shaped
from braided steaks, hide
cinched & pulling everywhere
like a badly tailored
Flesh Dress, these

flattop boys of tribalism
with facial hardware
& blue-algae
garlands of tattoo—

All of them, every one,
scraping & toe-touching
to pick up the gourmand's trail

because on a man
in his fifties, it's money

what rips.

Behold then the ravenous
entrepreneurs of lean mass, & a parking lot
full of Beemers.

iii.

A gilt Hermes & Hephaestus
lean on doric columns
        flanking the juice bar
to sip shakes of creatine & whey.

Goons lay down
in longshoreman toques
to bend a bar
with the weights they bench   (black
                        plates flanged
                        like the bulkhead stoops
                        on a ship)
& their ropy
quadriceps,
                thicker than cables
to tether a tanker, taper
over the bench end, denim shorts gaping
inside the thigh.

Sex trade workers
whisper to cell phones
in the co-ed
steam room.

And gang heavies spot
for a warlord, doing squats, whose
buddy's brains
spread across a dancefloor
& the local papers
last month.

iv.

Among these
mandarins & courtesans
I would be lying
not to report my
collaborationist
allegiances.

Younger women
with studded navels
train in tandem. A separate
peace? Others yet
march as ghost legions

grey, translucent skin
on the step machines:

lightly leaning
on spun-glass forearms
& ready to die
or revenge us
by a resistance
that diminishes
&
diminishes.

V.

I hate this place
but have found no better way
to hammer out my days.

Axiomatic
[*sic*]:
the body hums with ungrounded static.

In the beginning was the Nerve,
nebulae of synapse
in black space, a toneless
pulse, pro-
       prioceiving
nothing &
          nothing &
               nothing &

The Bang's echo a background madness
that buzzes like a transformer in the chest.

Born to a panic, airless
& electric, & exercise
kills it, fills the bellowed ribs
for a day. Endorphin
mystic, bowed under
by frenzy, drink lambency
from oxygen, seek moments
of apotheosis
in the blood's crack-head rush.

What else have you got, shamans,
alchemists of meaning, humanists?
Show me.
What else have you got?

Gymnasia
make me

an auto-
chthonous
church.

Or, if the centre is void

this treadmill of effort
a vaudeville complicit

"personal activism"

& the phallus recedes
as we chase it

(Proteus)

If what depth there is, is
surfaces, is
water's writ, is

quicksilver? If that

is the only legend
with credence among the elements

(Affirm *anything*—

        still the proteins
              extend a certain furlough
        from the sea.

The Hedonists

We ride the stationary bike
every day, forty-minute sessions, our cheeks
flushed to pink
like a salmon & red pepper
alfredo.

Rounded, human, on the scales
of rigour & good living
we break even.

In grey fleece, we clip
sweat-brittle
back issues of *Gourmet*
over the red-eyed
digits of the display screen

our headphones ablast
with the *Ode to Joy.*

Gin & Tinned Fish

Take your zinc w/
pineapple juice, derek says,
for the girlfriend—
that combo delivers
a bigger, sweeter load

Get your protein from food
when you can; powder
supplements, derek says,
give you gas

*—But the night munchies
are ruination
when you're in training*

Gin & tinned fish, he says,
that's a man's weight-loss plan
for bedtime;
I'll write a book about it

tuna w/ mustard
or fatless whey
sweetened w/ aspartame
only if you're in a rush

& enuf Gordon's
& sugarless tonic
to kill the pangs
leave you snoozing
—totally KOed—
five minutes
after sex

(Bodybuilding
is the big man's
anorexia

& a lover
lying alone, beside you
in the dark

part of the diet.

One of the Guys

in the office, Derek, firks out a Polaroid
of last night's stag, somebody's
body, splayed & dis-
played, foreground, as a scrum
of wolf-eyed goons
tugs on her flanks & the smashed
groom, beer in his fist, cold
condensation at her bra-strap, celebrates
like a Shriner with a Florida marlin

his love for one woman. The photographer
is a bodybuilder, of certain clients he remarks
It's throttlin' time, & I grin
with him, say Hey, wanna train me on the Round Base Jammer
after work? Once I had a politics

but now I want to get ripped
cut & tremendously huge
in the manner prescribed by Joe Weider's
four magazines. Like Chamberlain or Zelig, like
Dorothy's snorting lion, I desire
the record to show me
both comical & well-liked. Daily
I work so hard to pass
among the other men
(*How about those Leafs*)
that I become one, & the poem is nothing
the poet nothing
but a late, lazy officer
who squats beneath the fixtures
with his binder & pen
to pad the public draft of a duty log.

Bankrupt

You can always tell the unemployed guy
says Fred at basketball—
he's the one in the best shape

not humped & pouchy from desk days
hollow shouldered &
weeble-hipped like a kangaroo
pawing the mousepad

but invested with muscle
a waist that flares upward to wide, amber lats
like a sleeve glass of ale.

Body is the one certainty
when all you have is time
for the gym

& no bank can garnishee
blood from the stone
you are.

Locker Room

And now, unveil'd, the Toilet stands display'd ...
—Alexander Pope

Optic

Every morning, the same bodies.

The twisted, over-
arching diligence
of men
soaping their buttocks.

Even the squat,
the bulging & molded
hardbodies
with abs flat
as landing strips

display modesties
in the shower: spin

to show you their backs
as you spin, frontal
to rinse lather from yours

—a furtive choreography
to avoid looking, or
          (everybody says so

to look while not looking
which is the locker room's
singular art, its

open secret:

To absolve
each man the other
of sight.

*

Olfactory

The smells their bodies make, & when,
their habits of scrubbing
gelling & brushing
& the complex
life of the masculine bowel

—circling like packdogs before sleep—

or after
shaving, a lingering
thru atomized
citrus notes
of Eternity, Égoïste, a discord
of zests, the whole
spiced & minty
toilette.

Equine
ammonium
at the urinals—
            standing naked
beside a guy
in a lifting belt.

Air of burnt protein
as Mr. Seventies
dries his mophead
at the wall-mounted
blower.

Like family, like roomies, I know
each man in this nameless corps
by musk & spoor
in private

down to the skin.

*

"Jaromir"

is a techie I recognize
from Systems,
lanky, with bad
rock-star hockey hair

& a horsy,
      tapering,
            uncut dick
that dances like a dropped rope

as he bursts from a stall
in a puff of his own vapour

& hits the showers
at 8:11

just as I do

(each knowing by the other
he won't be late.

*

Epic Simile

Just as Perseus
backing into history
with his mirrored concave of shield
dared encounter the Medusa's
snaky tendrils
only in reflection, so does

our hero, by inversion, check out
the other guys' cocks
in the buffed steel
back panel
of his locker door.

On hinges, it's adjustable, just as
he believes
he is, & one day he will face
what he cannot today

head on
& hardening like a stone.

*

Enlarger

Heavy
footfall, bone
on concrete;
the dainty
slap of toe pads &

squeamish kisses
as the skin peels free
with each step. Mincing

muscle-bound over tile
with a snarl & shoulder towel
to the showers: stiff
with a shampoo bottle
dangled at the navel for shy
hiding & sleight
of hand. No matter

how hard he pumps, how
thick & vascular
the extensor grows, his soft
centre lolls
immovable: un-
monstrous, & not half
the injustice

every man decries it. To
compensate, you will say,
for the lotus, he diets
& depilates, he jacks the iron—

It's death to flowers:
the whole torso
a lubed, riven head,
glans of the pecs.

Bashful & vicious
with arms crossed
low at the wrists, he
douches his foamy neck, he

fucks the very air
just by standing there.

*

Derek

bent over
in the two-step
scuttle: capillary

webbing of the bag
as it balloons,
behind;

elastic straps
primp the under-
curves—

& he stands, snaps
the band, jiggles
the pouch &

looking up
bloodshot, glowers
like a baited bear.

Uh-oh.

       "Hey," I grunt.

       Pause. Quizzical
       tip of the head.

       Satisfied, he huffs, "Hey"

turns back to his dressing
& I can breathe.

My desire for a man
is a thought bubble

    (slavering mad
    & cacophonous)

that soundlessly pops when he speaks.

Eyeplay is pure
cloak & dagger, life & death, Valentino

till the blood, dispelled
by a word

floods
into nothing at all.

Outage

One morning a circuit-breaker blew
& the showers went black, the glow of red EXIT signs
too feeble to see by, & the usual bevy of jocks & managers
had to feel their way
out of ridgy, tiled cubicles & along
paint-pebbled walls
to their locker doors. With bumps & soft excuses
they probed the gloom with fingers
to find or forfend
the flesh of other men—

but touched anyway, by accident, rubbed hips
or tingled at the fine brush
of forearm hair, the moist nap of towel
& skin, until one of the serious builders

dug out a flashlight, more or less
for his own use, & needled his knotty quads, one
by one, thru the elastic thighs
of his Joe Boxers. All we could see
were his bright parts, brief snapshots of gym bag
& shampoo, sternocleido mastoid
& chin, as his beam jittered round the room
like a firefly, his stylus illuminating
fragments of everything we knew
about this intimate place—it was

like camping with other boys
in a tent, whole galaxies outside
but the familiar
rustling & smells within, & then
just as our animal pupils
had pooled wide to the wilderness
of getting dressed for work
in the predawn, the power

came back, buzz
& flicker of fluorescents, like
a monster roused from the dead
luminosity tore a blanket from our bodies
& we captured one another, rumpled
armature of the masculine
discarded to the corners like the partyclothes
of a sober Sunday morning—

one man seated on a bench, stretching his exquisite toes
& toweling his calf like a dancer
who draws up a black stocking
while another
slapped puffs of talcum to his belly & groin
in an open stance, chest billowing forward
without shame. As though
for the first time
we saw one another, moviegoers
when the lights go up, so many men now
with scrubbed heads, our raw wet faces, we
blinked like babies, not hunched or preening
in postures of compensation
but standing
distracted, like a coven of Davids
in the solitary, low-slung nudeness
thick shadow had allowed—

& then that tableau, too, faded
into motion, & we hooked our towels, snapped ourselves
taut in the starched
mantle of public bodies, &
joking, whistling, birthed, burst
out from change room doors, knowing nothing of the dark, into the day.

Line Jumpers

Another person's narcissism has a great attraction.

—Freud

Man

Soft, man.

Put your head down

your shoulders apart

& to the aspirant
heart of the animal

listen.

breath measures

—& we are touching
for the first time, & what do i mean, line break
by the *first* time, i am pressing my face
into her sunburnt neck, her scarf & skin, i am breathing her in, deeply, at length, by
—preposition—
reflex

—like a hungry thing, snorting almost, ampersand
& inspired, *inspiring,*
pheromonal
or narcotic i am
drawing her into my lungs, my veins, hypo-
tactic like a line, a powdered line, a line on a mirror, a metaphysical line in a blue wig

like a simile

—all for fear
that i will never hold her again.

my company has authorized me to say,
never write a poem that is about wanting the wrong person
inside your person

—wanting her entirely inside my person, write O

apostrophic O, delirious cheerios

O/ like a long & inelegant, comma, unbreathable line

a line for nine-litre lungs, hey charles O, i blew the inky wands off the spirometry paper &

                                                        jitter-
                                                                    bugged
                                                    in the crinkled
                                                                    margins
                                                of science
                                                                            O

my chest x-ray, big boy, my coiled & ruled rib cage was too capacious for one
                                                        [photographic plate

(so take two)

(& make romance))

—O nothing, not even
the moral syntax of family, lyric closure
can measure, can break /
this hyperventilated, this fated, this gap-toothed & gorgeous

progression to her mouth, which is a line [theme! O

        nothing can stop me
        from kissing you now.

Medea

When he kissed the other woman
under Orion's dagger on the beach
his past went nova & burst upon him.

They say it takes four years
for a marriage to expire
once you've thought its ending.

For the brilliancy of a dead star shines
on & on across the placid galaxies
with millennia-old fire, outliving

itself & watchful as a jealous
god, an eye's pinprick upon the waves.
And a posthumous love reflects itself

with an echo of that big beginning:
a false bang, fool's gold, a flying ship
& revenge with the speed of light.

Breach

In fields of pack-ice miles across
there is a window through which you may breathe
& then
there is not.
            On winds, currents, over
this jade murk, floes
drift in patterns
that are mapped:
this open water may recur

       & may not. Narwhals
       cluster here & click
       tributes to their arctic
       lungs that abide
       even salt & ice.
             Breathe
now,
   they sing in morse—
& clatter in sparring
with soft-serve
tusks:

     Let the beluga
     or the bowhead
     feed. Baleen is indeed

       judicious
       if choice may be achieved
       by sifting.

     But next spring,
     in this same latitude
     fissures & futures

will seal over, the floes closing
in a white eclipse
to cap our unicorned heads.

      All then will be numb, all aching
      with cold, all a drowning
      amid years, & the idea of years.

As you rise into your falling,
trust the submarine noises
that you hear. One vision
echoes back to you: sound itself

      prophesies what is solid
      & reports the shape of things lost
      or things to come.

            Desire is the will's sonar.
            By voice you locate
            the skin of the sea
            & arch into its touch.

Polynya: that gap,
that crack in the icy dome
offers you air, a whole drifting
sky of it, & you may decide upon your surfacing

once.

Narcissa

like that postcard of the woman
straddling a dolphin

luxuriant with fingers
thru her own spray of hair

you tipped a shoulder back & met
your face in the dressing mirror, black

flapper cut in wet
sprigs against your forehead

your brash & gappy teeth
pickets of paperwhites as

scintillant, swaying, shuddered
you dragged

a palm across your breasts:
    I look beautiful, you said

& I, wanting only to act
your glass, your image to splash

on my body's flat pool
to the verge, agreed—

        You do
                you do
                        you do

—sounded lowly
& rippling beneath you, in your spring.

Eclipse

Leaves helix
      in little galaxies
around the wheels.

From the highway
      cut thru dogwoods:
a windshield full of stars.

Witness this moment
to tinted systems, he will leave
the one sphere he has charted

to visit Prospero's
island with you. Or some such curio
so miraculous: to nuzzle

the plummy oval
of a moon's shadow—silky on the jawbone
oiled & utterly

anointed.
One Uranian's
favourite thing: to climb

with every muscle of his face
the dome of liquid
nightsky. What need

other coordinates?
He is yours, blinkered
by your orbit. Miranda

obscures the far-off
tease, an ember or orchis
tucked beyond. The future's

corona, its wand & its
firebrand: between that sun &
what's here, there is nothing else he can see.

Mirror Mirror

We cannot decide
to take it down, the silver
platter of glass
wedged between the mattress
& the wall. We love
those two people, we say, such dishes
shimmering beside us in their pool
of mercury, our

best friends, so lithe &
horizontal, we are always so happy
when they come round

all they do is fuck, really, &
we like that about them.

Feminist Dad

Saturday morning, he took a breather
halfway thru a long jog
& made love to a woman not his wife
in her apartment by the seawall.

They argued on the threshold
as he forced his feet back inside
his cross-trainers.

Saturday afternoon, he spotted his son on left wing
thru wired glass
then called her from a payphone
near the concession, other dads
in traffic around him.

Fries too hot, he bargained
across the wires, eating
greedily, burning his tongue, greasing
the receiver & when

his wife & teething baby
split the swinging doors of the arena
with their wagon train of stroller,
diaper bag & detritus

he kissed her cheek
with his wet, busy, dog-stupid mouth

while the men smiled—
                              we turned
& smiled at her
& then we turned away.

Line Jumper

I'm happy
so long as we get better seats
than the line-jumpers, quips a droll boy, jester

beneath the marquee, as she & I
spin like two reels, threaded
at the fingers, & neither wavers
to eye the eyes of the ushers—onward

past the box office & thru
porthole doors
with other ticket holders, the ones
who queued under umbrellas, not singing

while we ate sushi across the street
& tingled with the scintillant drizzle
wasabi made
across the myelin sheaths of our brains—

What I wouldn't give right now
for a cream pie, says the clown

as we glide like celebrity's ghosts
down the escalator, tall creatures
buoyed by the fishy juices on our skin

then dance the mirrored foyer
in the nauseating, you know,

(ii)

vanity of straight romance.
My therapist says
I should find a more affirmative way
to tell my story, after all
we've broken no law with a name but

the crowd is already sick
of us, a mob scene
of tisks & scowls, just as

my lineage, shadow-relations, even my *droogies*
gaped helpless, no torches coming to hand, when

one year ago
I escorted my children
to play with her child, & found exile, nakedly
re-cast under cover of darkness
behind the screens
of this woman's parlour, I placed my mouth upon her sex

& my ears were sluiced by the perfect knowledge
of change, my past parting like a zipper
without due process, courtship or marriage, we

laid our own space
in the theatre of lovers
making lives, *normal*, & we claimed the best seats

(iii)

in the house, I declare it loudly
by this line, Doctor, like buskers in the road
we advertised our scandal by megaphone

(tho frankly nobody gave a damn)

& then ran for a future we knew
was the only script we were born to shoot

—Yes we set our palms flush
in the flicker of sunlight
thru a curtain
            (dustmotes, snowflakes, etc ...
to braid the traceries there

& we appealed to the lyric
value of intensity, which is

a disorder, after all
there are only so many
Loves-of-my-Life
a poet can name, without blushing

            (help me here, reader)

—We knew we were right
eventho it was wrong;
we would house a new cinema
of spliced footage & family &

            however you cut it

                (I was cured all right)

I jumped the whole bloody line of them

                                        to join her.

Miranda Spice

mirror mirror, admired Miranda, i want to trace myself in the glass of your grace &
drool pure anglophilia, dub my lines in your kentish tongue, i want to have & to be
you, by postural graft, your regal sashay, to walk your way, riding-crop sway in your
arms & hips & the bronze, upright miles of your dorsal ridge.

the public school whose uniform you wore bore sackville-wests in the roll call, & we
toast anniversaries at knole house to seal a doublet love of orlando.

(in the photos, we are bounding across the mounds of the deerpark.)

my kids cannot decide if you look more like sporty or posh, but i know your team
practised archery, shoulder to shoulder with Diana's school, & i imagine you with her,
in the blue eyeshadow 70's, bending a huntress bow together.

Then one summer day she dies & we cynics grow tragical, suddenly chummy with that
classmate we'd teased. You thirty-six, a mother like her & feeling it that way, my
Ex- thirty-six & also so wrecked,

she scolds my plummy phrasing
of your name in this mournful context:

> You've even started to *prance* like her, she says,
> so i say, Call it what you will it's exquisite,
> & she says, Sure, on a wannabe princess maybe, not on a man,

& i wince, all two metres & fifteen stone
buckles a little, thinking on the obvious *matter* of me
in your bedside mirror, Miranda—that slab
of my torso & hams
flexing the wishbone of your thighs

—that hairy back of a caliban, a colony's beast
who whispers to women his wish, his oh just sometimes wish
to glide on slender legs with small, slippered feet.

Popular Culture

The day Ginger Spice™ quits the band
my four-year-old grrrl sings
If you wanna be my lover, you gotta get rid of my friends
into the microphone
of her swamp-water Slurpee™
from the back seat of the white
collision repair car
that says COLLISION REPAIR CAR
in red fender decals
to the drivers behind me, & replaces for this week
the broken, time-shared Saturn™
with bent rings & frame
that my ex-
drove over a cement retainer
after we fought with cinnamon faces again
over the break-up of our group.

Early in parenthood, with a curried flush
of the right politics
still swelling our lips

in the late eighties
when it was all soft men, eco-fem
& fealty to Tracy Chapman, who taught us
to doubt our desserts,

                    we vowed
there would never be war
toys, postmodern
cleavage or the word
custody. There would be time enough
for voices in benevolence
& the hand-washing of Enfalac™ tins
for flattening into the blue box.

Meanwhile our world bloomed with vibrant children
like an agar plate.

As I am boiling over Kraft™
mac & cheese, my son
pumps up his Super Soaker CPS 1100™
straps it across his back like a flamethrower
& blasts a jet across the driveway
at a bigger kid
shooting hoops, who grabs the collar
of my boy's Goosebumps™ t-shirt
& strips him of the water rifle
in a second

—which is less time than it takes me
to launch my grown-up body
across the kitchen
                          & over the patio fence
to shout the thug down
with flailing arms & sweat in my eyes
as he prepares to fire
& the other parents of the evening gaze on
knowing I am no crazier
than we all are, however it may look.

My new partner suggests I'm a little tense
because we've not made love™
(she uses other words
not permissible in a poem™
written for television)
in almost three days, & that I am really
no different from other men™

—however else
I told her our new world would look.

Signet

For we who have vowed & broken there is
a perjury in love's superlatives.
I want you as closure's invert couplet;
& tho I twice cried wolf, you are the wolf
to devour my dessert days—a pledge set
in type again despite use. In the gulf
between what I've contracted & might now
lies shame's flat calm: what lyric can I give
who has left a betrothed bereft & low
with her book of tributes & years to live
free of me, *hypocrite auteur*, elect
to have pressed mettle to either & spent
of the soft-wax oaths I would now select
to seal with you in faith?

                    That letter's sent.

Post

A slow postcard from Genoa
wonders if my wife is well. Your
name still scars the aorta
of a blood-rust arbutus

trunk. The Sister from up
the lichened bluff
brings sprigs of forsythia—
dead in a carafe. Your yellow

letters, budding with promise,
shuffle in a candy box. In dreams
the lover beside me now
unveils your face, a Barnum

hoax. Blossoms split, sunbright yet clipped
from the old source. In his casket,
the Sister boasts, Frère André's nails grew
without a ghost.

Wedding Dance

Artifice, the crystalline
& serene meniscus
or killing pool of the sea: to bathe as animals
next to such inert *techne*,
the martini-chilled Atlantic & that glittering ark
of culture, paralytic in a calm, electric lights & ice, you
can hear plashing, paddling
& children's voices
as though across a northern lake, with cabins, in Quebec—

to slip quietly
into aquamarine, a death by Lawren Harris
sweetened with strings, their plectra
of half a million bones
in pirouette on the prow
of jeweler's vainglory;
to die there in time
& watch it happen, clockwork, an engineer's certainty
there will be a flatline dawn:
these are the conditions,
that was the forecast,
this is the wedding dance—

To know for those gala hours
the way I know today, that all
I relish & devour, the very
red ink in my veins
as I jog the deck of the world,
will be spilt—like the decanted
sherry that shudders
on the mantel—& I will molder
in draperies of dark, sunken & stripped
of what I never possessed
& clamber to keep
even in the dead, rived

centre of this minute
I believe I am soaring, & seen, & alive.

It's an ad
for *vanitas* &
everybody's in it, the mind's
vital cheat against the mind, its
fingernail grit
down the beloved spine
of loss. What they want,
these greedy teenagers, as they sweat
in the hold, as they scale the upright stern
that slides to nothingness
beneath them—& they are right—is not *ennui*
but this: To draw
the full salt spume
from each posthumous second we are given, in stark
foundering excess, beneath the billion ice-water stars, with you.

Perfect

That eighties movie with Jamie Lee Curtis & John Travolta as
an aerobics instructor dating a gonzo *Rolling Stone* journalist
is bad in myriad ways, & it is only meet that Travolta served ten
years in obscurity for this lapse of judgment. We guffaw at the
video, our embarrassment as cheesy hets make do-me eyes to
an ur-techno beat & Curtis pivots her fleshless pelvis in a humping
squat. Well it is meant to be sexy but you feel like a med student
in the theatre of Anatomy.

All my adult life I have courted anxiety disorders, OCDs, & now
I talk like the anorexics my partner treats as a psychiatric nurse.
Miranda comes home after a twelve-hour shift & I give discourse
upon the relative fat grams in a can of tuna vs. three tofu wieners.
She twitches, stares me down over the bowl of Häagen-Dazs she
administers as an antidote to this ethos I am swallowing whole.

Daily I am growing thinner & cutting off my hair. Miranda fancies
the skinhead look because Desire rebels against the softer self,
because of the National Front, because I now resemble her Aussie
ex- & the common yobs her mum hated when she was a teenager
in the gentile green belt of Kent, circa 1978.

Perfect Form (w/ Clinamen)

Foods can be categorized as clean & unclean according to lipids
content. After Whitman I use the word *perfect* in whatever I write
then cross it out. I know that the perfect body is a futurist dream
& ruse, I know that *futurist* is an aesthete's euphemism for fascist.
What difference does it make what I know. I abhor every letter & ort.

Every odd remainder.

The speaker of the poem is chronically constipated despite a heavy
ingestion of bran & fibre supplements. His weight-training regime
is based on an encrypted system of reps & exponential super-sets,
& these lines, though they look like prose, are in fact standardized by
a gaunt numerology of leading & type. If they grow longer or erratic
as the piece clenches its cheeks toward closure, attribute this change
to his hunger for thoroughness, above all. He introduces a little, oh, raggedness
post-facto, to pass himself off as *healthy*. This book is perfect bound.

Dumbhead

*Do not ask who I am and do not ask
me to remain the same; leave it
to our bureaucrats and our police to
see that our papers are in order.*

—Michel Foucault

whatever pumps him, he plays

on the headphones
in the gym. billy idol, dumbhead metal, even
zz top: chainsaw guitars, the musky

mewling & yowl of *Legs*
soothe the lizard brain as it presses iron.
vertigo of
who am I without a woman
to be inside? panicked
reptile sleeps only here, flexing a heavy bell, or there

when he has entered her. peace

is there, essential blank
of the organism. there
is home & feels like
purpose, elemental.
(never without
a regular girlfriend
since sixteen: one of the badges
of cowardice he boasts of—

knees bent to a half-squat
behind her
as she pegs
her elbows to the sofa: spreads
her undercurves to watch *himself*
diminish, vanishing
into—& the lizard exhales
with the warmth of closing
folds / lifts
for a moment
its sticky fingerpads
from the brainstem, & every choice
the man has ever made.

what would his life, this island be, without?
meaningless, hisses
the despot with a tongue flick, *head*
      full of noises
                (in the vacuum of space

& *not an outed sound.*

Dumbhead II: Idle Idol Idyll

To the peace that comes of entry

he compares the silence
of a burial chamber

unsealed in the pyramid, or the
himalayan hush & foot-scuff

of the Lady chapel at Ely,
its idols broken & powdered

by frost on a December
noon; or the draftless chamber

of a tomb among the catacombs
(you raise a slab of stone & stir

dust that has settled for a thousand years.)
To the calm a woman gives he compares

the mute & subaquatic
wad of air in middle ear

that threatens madness in parking
garages, where pillars & ducts

swaddled in foam
muffle the soles & breathing

of bandits or *b-boatmen*
who squat with spring-loaded thighs

in wait.

Dumbhead III: Woman as Limit

he makes of each woman a border
to the livable world. his changeable
fidelity a shield
to the unknown, the new, she contains
the panic in his chest,
the groin, the aching triceps, if not
this one then another, mrs
or mistress, ok
always keep two women said
benny williams to
louis armstrong, ready nurses
to the overflow, the anxious gush
of essence, bullbody's
binding bull, its specious
species agenda, a gentle
pressure on the daily wives
to squeeze a man inside
a confined place
the way a newborn
sleeps with head wedged
into the corner of the crib
because cranial pressure
from the pelvic cavity
is uterine memory, because
a woman is the whole outside world
turned inward, a draperied room
of bone, involuted
surface that carries his myth
of edges, of small, eventho he knows
libido is limitless
by constraint, his whole sexed
being a water bomb
dissolute, vertiginous
& a man might easily vanish
as fluid into other fluids, ether, he needs
the tight space of a woman

as a second skin
to keep his insides in,
his blood from billowing out
                & into

(Choit la plume)

       the sympathetic blood
           of other men.

+

YOU USED TO WORRY YOU'D NEVER HAVE SEX. NOW YOU WORRY WHEN YOU DO.

You have good reason to be concerned. The possibility of contracting HIV is definitely more troubling than whether or not you'll "score," but such are the times we live in.

THE TRUE TEST OF YOUR MANHOOD. Fortunately, there's a simple way to arm yourself with knowledge: the Home Access Express™ HIV test system. In fact, it's the same test use an

anonymous code gives you exclusive access to your test result Additionally, you can call for confidential counseling 24 hou a day, 7 days a week. Counselors are available to give you advi about treatment offer

—Advertising copy for the
Home Access Express™ HIV 1 Test System
(Muscle & Fitness, February 1997)

122

Dumbhead IV: HIV as Limit

+ in which the pronouns shift

Flirting with guys in the gym
is a bad idea. Now that he
believes I am safe, muscle queer,
bi-tease, or at least
not a basher, he is
on me every day, I look up
from the abs mat
& he has been watching me
do crunches

He calls me a cyborg
& is sharper witted
than awkward I

am: he makes
nasty cocktail chat
about contemporary art
by the upright row

*(All b-boatmen
are Grace Darlings to me ...*

says I am too cute
to be a campus secretary
& calls me the Aesthete
tho I feel thicker
than Maurice at Cambridge

(Wrong texte, my dear

—He is a medievalist, parchment
fetishist, an archivist
for the Library
scandalized that I stuff

123

runny notes for poems
into my sweatsocks
between sets

(not exactly acid-free
he protests
on behalf of my papers)

he is just my height
but deeper thru the chest
pes stranga guma
with a celtic armband
tattoo, a gold loop
thru the eyebrow's eyelet
an orange-stubbled chin &

he has a sore
or birthmark, like an ink-blot
at his throat
that has lasted the whole three
flushed & gushing weeks I have known him.

Dumbhead IV.ii: Interval (Between the Walls)

Section 1(a): Excuses, or "Theory"

> *Once sexuality can be read and interpreted in*
> *the light of homosexuality, all sexuality is subject*
> *to a hermeneutics of suspicion.*
> —Lee Edelman

homosex the rabbit he plucks from every hat:

Or, emblem of eruption
chasm he can probe forever:
smoking gun, The Clue, it is always true, a case file
rising to the moon, like magic it explains
WHAT IS WRONG WITH HIM, Or: *Inquirer,*
some quests are not sexual in nature
is a dumb show
& who reads lips?

Confessional verse
an exercise in the liar's paradox:
compulsion is my theme
he said, four times.

     (mind hiding
     inside a Trojan)

       (he blows like St. Helen's)

Just keep telling him, she laughs later,
you're in love with this beautiful woman.

Dumbhead V: Plovers' Eggheads

Once I gave a reading
in this weight room

& my Archivist
loves the newsphoto
of these snarling pit-bulls, lips
& sleeves peeled back

—reminds him of that scene
in *Brideshead:* one
of the vice-regent boys
delivers with lisp & stutter
The Waste Land
by megaphone
to the sweatered and muffled throng
of rowers at Oxford

then retreats from the balcony
for a Cointreau

(but I am his dunce,
his stenographic hunk, no
longer scholarly, clark
not clerk, I am red-faced,
he is my Blanche, & whatever oiled
postures of erudition
I strike here

—are retroactive.

Dumbhead VI: Shaved Head Passes
in Cannon Beach, OR, or
the Panic Defence

The innuendo, poetry boy, is slanderous &
as storytelling,

salacious: ominous
suggestion, so delicious

to straight culture, the scare
of gay contagion, it was just

a shaving blemish, a purplish
brownish, forked, smudging, blade-hickey

& it went away, it went away (&
even if it didn't / I needed that

imaginary sarcoma there
to close the question marked

in the curve of a lycraed ass
—to soothe the split hysteria

prissy & stigmatic
harbinger of the blood blot

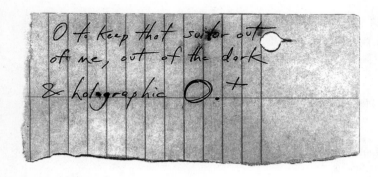

O to keep that suitor out
of me, out of the dark
& holographic O. +

+

Last August
he got his scalp buzzed
with No. 1 clippers
& travelled thru the States
under the changed eyes
of strangers, hotel clerks, he was obviously
not a military man
so with that skull, that bristly
pencil-sketch of hair, he was obviously

working out in an upscale gym
with bottled water & a whale mural
in Cannon Beach, hippie
town with the tightest lips
on the whole left coast, he was

O Homo
-chondria of the closet class
& I am its
valedictorian.

    —& exactly which part
of real suffering
is it
that you envy?

sweating up the machines
after a jog from Haystack Rock
& looking bony, his granite temples
shot with veins, his white
T-shirt in the wall mirror, he was

lifting in a circuit of sets
& wiping off each seat or grip
with towels & disinfectant spray

but still a fellow traveler
in fitness, a hidebound
marathoning type
worked in
on the leg press,
the incline bench
cocked a different spray bottle
held her breath
inside a grim face

& positively
blasted the pads
again

& again

+:

to kill his every trace.

Sexing the Page

                         my derridean dissertation

    on the concrete poem
                as rebus
    for the hermaphrodite body

                         was never so real as

    the day my friend the archivist
                         with white cotton gloves
                         in the climate-

controlled vault

jerked me
                (me)   (me)   (me)
                                                   off

all   over   the
                              delicate

yellowed original

                    of bissett's

                    am/or

Thiefs Journal: Glottal Jack

(Courier-matrix 49 x 14)

Jong *je-nez*, eyeknows, Ma, death throws on death-
row. Broom flowers? Fish-you-all-eyes. Vishnu?
Play that tile or dis tile; distyle. *Disent-ils*.
Arche text, you're. Mechano. Domino no notions.
2 E-Z. The fasting nation of watutsi cult. Aet.
Gl—ahh. A dill. Doe. A female dear? Arraign,
Andropov's girlie son. Me? A name I gal myself.
(The trans ation is exa t. Oh knife, in shining:
amour? Sheath's log. Vanilla eyes. Aet a moll,
oh gee! Latin force. Cab bard. Taxi, scabbard.
Caught aux creases. (G)love. Petalpush pod-ner.
Hi men. Art, a tack. An T-erection. Anther me,
eagle, I, rebus, mark. Auf! he bung. Skingraft.
Stay, men. Style? Sex pistil. Anther me! Bud?

Dumbhead IX: Found Poem

So one day Miranda finds this poem

so far, face up on my desk
& appeals to our face-up
document rule
which holds that any exposed manuscript
around the house is free for reading, but
paper-shuffling
or the opening of journal pages
is prohibited—

Miranda finds this poem, so far
& although we both know better than to explain
I start to explain

Dumbhead I - XIII™ *is a work of fiction, & any*
resemblance of its characters ...

Dearly tested reader,
                        it is too late
to complain. You broke the rule, the seal, & the compact.
You peeled back the sheets, & every page you turn
hereinafter—

Dumbhead X: Seminal Text *

Camerado, this is no book,
Who touches this touches a man.
—Walt Whitman

---

*   Originally left blank to accommodate a watermark of authorial ejaculate, this page remains intact to preserve the integrity of the signature, against advice from counsel. Do not attempt to remove this leaf from its binding. Private inscriptions may be elicited from the poet.

      Alternatively, taxpayers are invited to fill this space with their own inconsequential drivel. After all, you paid for these resources, & the author is obviously wasting them.

Dumbhead XI: Essay on Marriage

What the Inquirer is trying to do, here, is allegorize
object exclusion & the loss
he cannot grieve.

Or: he is confusing the dissemination of text
with sleeping around. Paper is brave,
paper is promiscuous, to publish
is to play the field.
(He believes you are grasping him now, his

wank scholarship.

—*Truth is you don't need anyone,*
Miranda writes &

he admires: words that bind
to their own falsehood

silky as the slipknot
in a bedpost scarf.

Freedom-giving is an irresistible ruse.

> *I releash you,*

their little joke.

Advice Column

1) *A tergo poetica*, a slippage or sinking doubt in the mechanics, bar of white chocolate massage oil from Lush™ spread melting across the immaculate confection of gendered pronoun's object, you know it when you squeeze it, leavened loaves of androgyny versus kulchur's kneejerk PIVMO, cf. *The girl's all right (raow-raow ... raow ... raowraowraow)* & the poem as air-guitar workout, *passim*.

2) We each drew a map of the Domain of Personhood. We compared. We accused each other of tracing. We corrected for reflexes. We gave mutual ground.

(The secret is, we are using the same map. It bears the same symbols, the same legend, the same key. It is a map we each have drawn. It traces the Domain of Personhood.)

3) When we say I love you, it does not mean I want to annihilate, erase & rewrite you, tho we have been that route, & if it works for people, we wish them every contentment.

4) With Genet, we aver that betrayal is an ethical necessity. But we are lying about it.

Tho a husband boast to play libertine
mark it down to apotrope: needs her

so bloody badly
advertises his meat
market readiness
to muzzle the fearsome jaws of—

Men's Health says: buff enough
to forfend the whelpish
catastrophe of—

Alone.

COMME SI
    just any
        body will do.

The poem of betrayal is nothing
but a preemptive assault
on getting dumped.

You dumbhead: you dickheart.
You acolyte of the pectoral cleft.
You glans of the chest.

Dumbhead XII: Play Risk

If we strain thought clear of impulse slowly,
slowly the day scream subsides to ordered lust.
—Anne Carson

One lover as limit
to the utter, able world

    (back off i'm taken)

Erects his anorexia
of "life experience"

(that hard venous line
of phallus & forearm)

The sexual being
a lipogram, his posture of betrothal
a martial art:

    + *in short, I was unavailable.*

- To trim to perfection
with absolute exertion
a domain so cramped & trivial.

Bodybuilding, like the habit
of monogamy, is a controlled simulation
of a wilder aesthetic.

A walled city. Farmed vigour.
The Weider principles / for a wider back.

    (It's a nice day for a /
             white wedding.)

Serial fidelities
protect him
from choosing to do
anyone/thing
new.

> *Come for crantinis*
> *on my roofdeck*
whispers the Archivist.

The eye's banquet
of fresh lovers
     as he grinds out his reps
a substitute for writing.

A CUTIE DATE

A substitute for faith.

> *We'll eat smoked eels*
> *from Amsterdam*

A substitute for hang-gliding
cleaning the toilet
meditation:
     for volunteering at the hospice
or feeling the full present
     of her singular love.

> *& toast the sun's red*
> *infusion*
> *with the sea.*

Exchange
phantasmal desires
for tasks.

Obscenely methodical.

Not another fuck
but another book.

It's a nice day to
start again.

•

                        The political self
                        —abdicates—
                        & he gets Hard.

Desire is boundless *And.*

The act a slave to limit
act a slave to limit
a slave to limit
slave to limit
to limit
limit.

•

Adultery as a vocabulary
for bold action

SHAM, EH?

is pretty lame. Is colloquial. Is bathos. Is prose.

(Flirtation's frippery
comes easily
'cause he's
Always Already Married.

+: As if sleeping with new continents of bodies
is the same sum gain as

"risk"
(beyond the viral)

as travel
(to Irkutsk)

as courage as
bringing a range of potential selves
into un-
               (un coup de dés)
                             concealedness

global
openness
& make-a-mess

NOPE, HE'LL ERR, A

As if the endlessly renewable
new lover
is the true brink of hazard & growth
    poiesis
        making new
            on the cusp of the moment as if
clear-cutting the wilderness of other green & pulpy flesh

is not
more or less

LIZARD

    a nice start

    hisses
        Tiresias / despot

    with a tongue flick.

Dumbhead XIII: Bi

If the image of a man pass
thru the rims of a black hole & in—
but it cannot, the module of flesh passes
while the light that clothes his nameable self
snags on gravity, the hard pull that the dark takes
& the snapshot of a last ecstasy on this side, whichever
this side is, hovers there, blistered to the lip of history, to shine on
even if the body of the man be far gone (in) or come out
already, wherever in is / out is, the rays of knowing
him, or thinking so, hung to fade on choice's
cusp—& we scorn his flicker, wave fists
in the air yet cut with no shadows
a picture of one who is neither

there nor there

Acknowledgements

The author gratefully acknowledges the Canada Council for the Arts, the BC Arts Council, & the Ontario Arts Council for their support of this project. Thanks also to Jeff Vaughn of the UBC BirdCoop; to Heather Cadsby & Maria Jacobs; to Michele Benjamin, Mike Harling, Sean Brooks & Kevin Brooks; to Alma Lee; to Pamela Banting, Kate Braid, Lorna Crozier & Gary Geddes; to rob mclennan; & to Denise Ryan, for coaching. Editorial thanks to Miranda Pearson, Esta Spalding, Ryan Knighton, Karl Siegler & Erin Soros.

Change Room is a work of fiction.

"Gulf Island Panic" first appeared in *The Moosehead Anthology: Forbidden Fiction* (1994) with "Hospital Greens," "[*sic*]" & a version of " **ur   limi t s**: Diagnostic." Wai Kei Lee produced "Hospital Greens" as a text object—adhesive labels on card stock with inset sacrospinal x-ray film—for the conference "On the H Orizon: bpNichol After Ten," Emily Carr Institute of Art & Design, Vancouver, BC, September 1998. "Home Ice" was produced as a poster by the National Museum of Scotland, Edinburgh, & anthologized in *Present Poets 2: Scotland to the World to Scotland*. "Dumbhead" was printed in *Capilano Review* 2:30 (Winter 2000). Other poems included here first appeared in *Arc, Canadian Literature, Geist, Malahat Review, Matrix, Prairie Fire, Quarry, Writers' Forum* (UK) & in the anthologies *Breathing Fire: Canada's New Poets, Thru the Smoky End Boards: Canadian Poetry about Sports & Games,* & *Written in the Skin: A Poetic Response to AIDS*. Thanks to the artists & editors involved.

"Bioluminescence" is for Wendy. "Wedding Dance" is for Miranda.

The invocation from Ovid belongs to Robin Blaser ("The Fire"). The epigraph from Mays is a kind of tactical obscenity; for context, see Frank Davey's *Canadian Literary Power*. "Game Theory" O-es something to Shari Benstock. Vancouver author Daniel Gawthrop wrote about Pavel Bure's lips before I ever did. In addition to the writers it quotes or mentions, "Dumbhead" cribs from Leo Bersani, Judith Butler, Michael Moon, Gayatri Spivak, & Erin Soros.